What Can I Make Today?

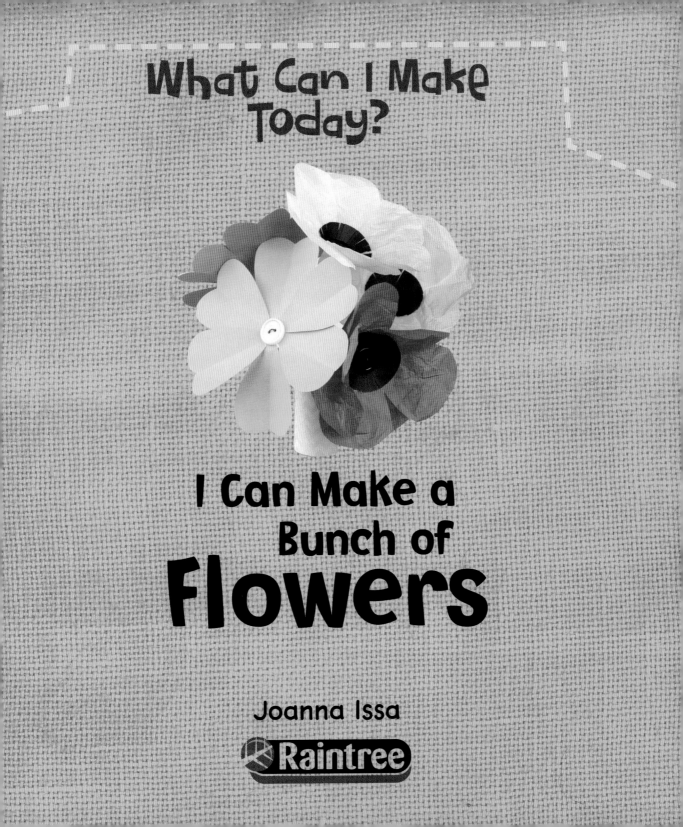

I Can Make a Bunch of Flowers

Joanna Issa

Raintree

Raintree is an imprint of Capstone Global Library Limited, a company incorporated in England and Wales having its registered office at 7 Pilgrim Street, London, EC4V 6LB – Registered company number: 6695582

Edited by Penny West
Designed by Philippa Jenkins
Picture research by Elizabeth Alexander
Originated by Capstone Global Library Ltd
Production by Victoria Fitzgerald
Printed and bound in China

ISBN 978 1 406 28403 4
18 17 16 15 14
10 9 8 7 6 5 4 3 2 1

British Library Cataloguing in Publication Data
A full catalogue record for this book is available from the British Library.

Acknowledgements
We would like to thank Capstone Publishers/ © Karon Dubke for permission to reproduce photographs.

Cover photograph reproduced with permission of Capstone Publishers/ © Karon Dubke.

We would like to thank Philippa Jenkins for her invaluable help in the preparation of this book.

Every effort has been made to contact copyright holders of material reproduced in this book. Any omissions will be rectified in subsequent printings if notice is given to the publishers.

Disclaimer
All the Internet addresses (URLs) given in this book were valid at the time of going to press. However, due to the dynamic nature of the Internet, some addresses may have changed, or sites may have changed or ceased to exist since publication. While the author and Publishers regret any inconvenience this may cause readers, no responsibility for any such changes can be accepted by either the author or the Publishers.

Contents

Some words are shown in bold, like this. You can find them in the glossary on page 23.

What do I need to make a rose?

To make the rose, you will need the rose petal **template**, pink paper, yellow paper, green **tissue paper**, two buttons, a **cotton reel** to draw around, **wire**, a **split pin**, scissors, a pencil and glue.

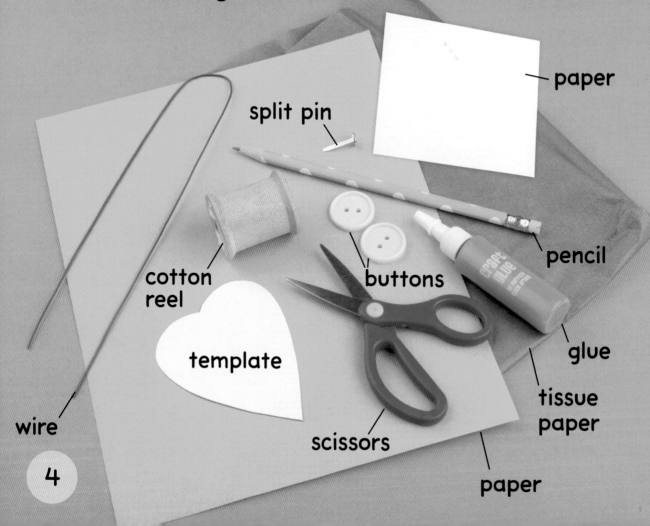

paper

split pin

pencil

cotton reel

buttons

glue

template

tissue paper

wire

scissors

paper

To make the template, photocopy page 22 and then cut out the rose petal shape.

paper

cardboard tube

To make the vase, you will need a cardboard tube, paper and glue.

Make the rose petals

Put the **template** on a piece of pink paper and draw around the shape six times to make six petals.

6

Cut out the petals, then fold
them in half.

Make the middle of the rose

Draw around the **cotton reel** to make a circle on the yellow paper. This will be the middle of the rose.

Cut out the circle.

Glue the petals around the circle.
Leave a small space in the middle of
the circle for a button.

Make the rose stem

To make a stem for the rose, make two holes in the middle of the circle with a **split pin**.

Put a button at the back of the rose and one at the front. Push the **wire** through the back button, the hole in the circle and the front button, so the wire goes through all three holes.

Ask for adult help

Bend the wire down, then push it back through the front button, the hole in the circle and the back button. Twist the wire tightly.

Ask for adult help

Cut a strip of green **tissue paper**.
Wrap the tissue paper around the
wire and use tape or glue to hold
it in place.

Now you have a rose!

Make the vase

To make a vase for the rose, cover the cardboard tube with coloured paper and glue it in place. You can make lots of roses or read on to make a different flower.

What do I need to make a poppy?

To make a poppy, you will need red and green **tissue paper**, the poppy petal **template**, black and green paper, **wire** and two buttons.

wire

template

buttons

tissue paper

paper

To make the template, photocopy page 22 and then cut out the poppy petal shape.

Make the poppy petals

Put the poppy template on red tissue paper, draw around the shape seven times to make seven petals, then cut them out.

Make the middle of the poppy

Cut out a small circle of black paper.
Make small cuts all around the circle.

Glue the petals around the circle.

Make a cone for the stem

Cut out a circle from the green paper. Cut a line from the edge to the middle. Twist the circle into a cone shape, then glue the sides together. Cut off the end of the cone.

Make the poppy stem

Follow the steps on pages 11 to 13 to fix the stem to the poppy. Push the cone up the **wire** and tape it in place. Wrap green **tissue paper** around the wire for the stem.

What can you make today?

You could make a colourful bunch of flowers for Mother's Day or a birthday present.

Flower templates

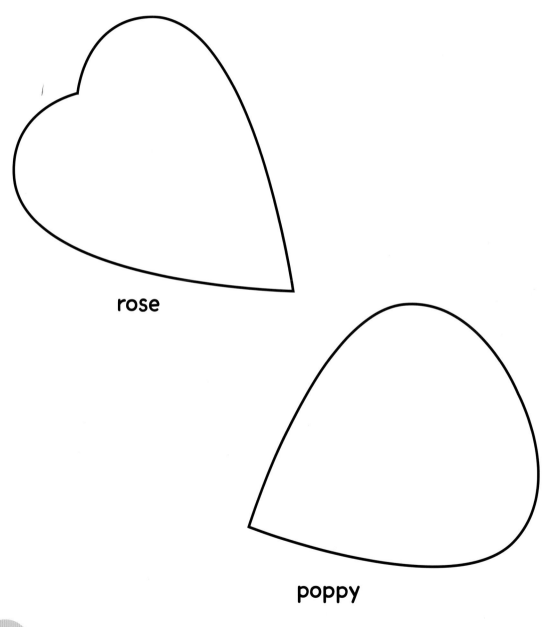

rose

poppy

Picture glossary

cotton reel small, round object that holds thread

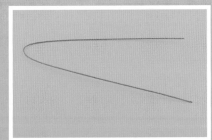

split pin metal pin with ends that bend

template pattern of a shape cut out of paper

tissue paper very thin paper

wire thin strand of metal that can be bent easily

Find out more

Books

Easy Origami Toys, Christopher Harbo (Raintree, 2012)

Having Fun with Paper (Let's Do Art), Sarah Medina (Wayland, 2011)

Red Ted Art: Cute and Easy Crafts for Kids, Margarita Woodley (Square Peg, 2013)

Websites

www.rhs.org.uk/Children/For-kids
A Royal Horticultural Society website where you can discover fascinating facts about plants and flowers.

spoonful.com/crafts
Visit this website to read about fun art projects, including easy flower crafts.

Index